book of common breath

book of common breath

poems by

d. ellis phelps

© 2026 D. Ellis Phelps. All rights reserved.
This material may not be reproduced in any form, published,
reprinted, recorded, performed, broadcast,
rewritten or redistributed without
the explicit permission of D. Ellis Phelps.
All such actions are strictly prohibited by law.

Cover image: "Suspended in Silence" by Esther van Overbeek

ISBN: 979-8-90146-711-4
Library of Congress Control Number: 2026935135

Kelsay Books
502 South 1040 East, A-119
American Fork, Utah 84003
Kelsaybooks.com

for my children

Acknowledgments

Gratitude to the publications where these poems first appeared:

Aries: "trees like children"

Central Texas Writer's Society Anthology: "wilderness"

Equinox: "holy water"

fws: international journal of literature & art: "breath of the cosmos"

poems2go: *"*crouch close to the fire*"* as *"every bone"*

the poet's billow: "before the dance"

Red Headed Stepchild: "uneven heat"

Texas Poetry Assignment: "multiples of seven"

Windhover: "when the last white line sails by"

Contents

Foreword: Breath Is Prayer   13

i. bittersweet

how do we speak of love	19
like no time has passed	21
like the time	23
uneven heat	24
dusk	30
trees like children	32
love is a curious creature	34
she is always	37

ii. body: meant to bend

ode to the breaking of day	41
determined wobble	42
before the dance	45
she let herself go	49

iii. breath becoming

common breath	57
two players	60
when the last white line sails by	61
holy water	63
multiples of seven	66

iv. unbroken

shape-shifted	73
to see or not to see	82
say this	84
supreme being	86
breath of the cosmos	88
blessing	90

Foreword: Breath Is Prayer

"Love is relationships.
Personal as pain and healing—
d ellis phelps's *book of common breath*
Opens the Lotus of her Art as Life—
from shopping to the heat of warmed hearts
From moon to bird and fox and mountain lion—
Shapeshifting trees into kids and dogs and cars
that demand a time for attention-like food!
Prayer is this Baptist dancer's personal saga
into self-acceptance. Music is here like holy waters.
Loss and Acceptance. Disturbance and Quiescence.
Stone and Fire. Stillness. Belief. Worship. Perception is
    Everything—
d. ellis phelps shares her Wildflowers freely. This is a
    Compendium—
of Everyday Miracles! Bless by Reading!"

—Spirit Thom, Texas Beat Poet Laureate 2020–2022

All these things shall love do unto you that you may know the secrets of your heart, and in that knowledge become a fragment of Life's heart.

—Kahlil Gibran

i.
bittersweet

how do we speak of love

my prince has come
wearing camo without a shirt

—not a penny in his pocket

we sit for hours
gambling at life

we do not dance
we do not kiss

like lovers

we are involved
in making

~

meanwhile   the rose
& all that   flat grass

tomatoes turned under
a pool—not splashing

this is not regret
but an open

—ended

question

~

how do we speak of love:

my head on your chest
your hand on my head

you—coming home

~

our breath
soft as down
—a comfort

not   thrown off
each spring

but   —enduring

every
season

like no time has passed

he thinks he is the boss—a rooster crowing
he's a hawk-eyed instructor on every subject
the how to place a chair just so   so the cold winter wind
won't blow in through the back patio doors guy

he's the master procrastinator who can't quite find
the time to replace the window stripping
or fold up his clothes or hang them
—just drapes them on doorknobs or bed posts

but really   you can ask my husband anything:
he's mister know-it-all
and if you insist   he's mister-fixit:
a pool pump/a mower blade/a stuck truck
and if he can't fix it   he's mister i've-got-a-guy-who-can

he is my macgyver   my google   my uber driver
my road captain: the one who knows every single
scenic backroad to nowhere but he knows where
every road goes   my guy is a pit-bull in a business suit
he's a white-haired hippie ruling his kingdom from
the yellow bucket seat on his john deer throne
—the clean expanse of his lawn excelled by no other
he's the silver heart charm dangling from my wrist
he's a handy hunk   a honey-throated charmer:
boundless   wildness
refusing to be tamed

& when he comes home   he has the key to my door
even after forty-five years   i still want him here and he knows it
no matter how long he sits watching nascars make left turns
or cheering those boys on to lose again
this man is the only silver-haired fox i want in my box
—even though that's not so hot anymore—
there was a time   i tell you   we were flames
burning each other up   and to this day   when he snuggles up
nuzzles the back of my neck from behind me   my knees go weak

like no time has passed at all

like the time

we slipped away
to drink champagne mid-day
in the backseat
of your baby-blue jeep
—it's glass packs rumbling

bodies on loan

how we heated things up
how wet i was
how you tasted of tin
on my tongue

how we devoured this
comfort we had no right to keep

but after the rumble
after the glass-packs
after the backseat
and a few flutes of you

i shattered

still   there are
pieces of me
i haven't found

uneven heat

i

today it's cloudy with a brisk breeze
the neighbors   burning leaves burning wood
—too much   smoke
—too much   burning

ii

in this house: more burning

i turn the air conditioner on/you turn it off

it's eighty-one degrees in here   i say
—degrees of heat   of exhaustion
it's only seventy degrees outside   you say
    as if this fact matters

smell of beer
smell of hate

curse   of heat

iii

i stand in the grocery line

holding seasoned asparagus
hot corn on the cobb
i've   passed on the halibut

because my pockets are empty

white-skinned   thin woman
behind me   fine hair
sheer   mint-green shirt
holding a sheet cake in her arms

want to set that here   i ask
i can hold it   she says
it's my work-out plan

iv

i stand in the raffle line
at the corvette show:

dripping sweat
donating ten
hoping to win

a guy next to me:
—no teeth   soiled baseball cap—
drops fat cookies wrapped
in cellophane on the bar in front of me

i've already eaten one of those
says the woman with him
—red scar on her throat—
they're 330 calories each

nah! i say
those are calorie free
today only

v

i stand in line to pay for my find:
a vintage suitcase: caramel brown
circa 1950   twenty-one dollars

in seconds   my mind has lined
the bag in fabric/vintage photos/dripping beads

hot flash!   i say
scanning the room for breeze
i find under the ceiling fan
hot flash   i say again
my upturned face   red
my shirt   wet with sweat

tangible age—substantial—having its due

the woman behind me   large
baggy arms   holding an amber vase:
*mine aren't flashes   they're spells
what do you mean*   i say
*i mean they last more than a flash
—they're s.p.e.l.l.s.*   she says

punctuating. each. individual. letter.
making certain   we understand

vi

leaving the show   i drive through
a nearby neighborhood

on the street: two redheaded children
seated at a table by the curb
on the table: two pitchers/cups/a ladle

i approach

the girl steps off the curb
holding up a pink sign

what do you have there   i say
lemonade & water   she says

how much is the water   i say
a dollar   she says

grinning

fortunately   my pockets
are not empty this time

and i   am thirsty

vii

today the air   is heavy
warm moist heat but no rain
not even a breeze   trees   do not sway

starlings
cardinals

sing

viii

hot fast wind: agitates the chimes   blusters through
the backdoor   arrives in long waves
the trees—a rolling green surf

one swallow tail flies low

sun high in the east   lights an empty sky

eight shoots   soon to be blooms
adorn the bow of the barrel   red yucca

plumes

high above   vultures
ride the thermals

ix

    & i   am aware
of uneven heat

of earth   turning

each   diffuse edge
each   slanted shadow

dusk

after Andrea Hollander

this is what we call
the time for roosting
when birds return to the trees
the trees stark forms staunch
against the waning light

this liminal space
between the day and the night

this is the time when humankind
come in from their doing
inhabit their caves
and light a fire

here the whippoorwill and the owl
begin their calling into the dark
these are the uncertain hours
when shadows claim and swallow
all that you thought you knew

now the fox and the mountain lion
—hunting
their nocturnal eyes
piercing   the veil

soon the dreamworld will resume
and what you have not learned
will return again and again

the moon will take hold of you
move your waters as she wills

and if you are lucky

you will find the only solace that comes
in the arms of someone you love

trees like children

dusk exhales   chills
stops me in the hall
outside the room
where i used to sing
my son to sleep

twisted together like
licorice sticks we'd tickle
and talk of dreams
banish under-bed beasts
plan how to deal
with dad and bless him

—this ritual assurance that
darkness doesn't bring death
that morning would wake him

his things: sorted and stored
left space for pines
uprooted from forest floor
and sentenced to ceramic for life

they wait in the corner
ask to be tucked in

imagining trees   like children
might be afraid of the dark
i turn the light on

recall my mother's soft soprano
singing brahms' lullaby
hear our whispers and prayers

remember how i held her hand
when she tried to go
wouldn't let her leave until
my father's voice called:
harsh   demanding
—ending assurance

dusk exhales   chills
imagining trees like children
might be afraid of the dark
i leave the light on

love is a curious creature

my husband says:

*if you dress like that
& hang out at tractor supply
you can find yourself a real man*

if he has passed on   he means
we talk this way often

this has to do with my
cinderella complex:
always losing that one shoe

it happens   mostly
after one of his spells
some of them   real
—brushes with death

i used to say
he was my knight
in shining armor
and i have spent
a lifetime   denying
this need for rescue

call it co-dependence
call it interdependence
call it partnership

but here is the truth:
—he is my sun
   i am his moon

& this is our universe:

~

singeing the walls with midnight fights
not-speaking—the silent treatment for days
going for counseling

telling each other every detail
of every happening
at the end of every day

toilet training three kids
house-breaking seven dogs
painting the stucco face of our hill-country home
battleship gray   burnt orange   gold
& once   on the inside: pepto-bismol pink

we've witnessed:

first teeth
first steps
first words

braces
pimples
bad perms

boyfriends
girlfriends
slumber parties
first dances
proms

the thrill of a first car
fade to the bittersweet moment
a child drives away

~

i've said:

i love you
i hate you
i want to leave you
i want you back
will you forgive me

& you have
every time

she is   always

love is a curious creature
that comes in the night—ransacking

the campsite   a thief   too
—she will steal   if you do not

secure what is yours

love is a shy creature
that comes in the night

chewing flesh   fresh vegetables
in neat rows

i have witnessed this

love is wild creature
that comes in the night

unkempt and wanting
panting with desire

refusing to be groomed

love is a winged creature
that comes in the night

perches on a branch
silent & still 'til dawn

—trusting you to feed her

some say   love comes
& love goes   but i say

this is not so
for if she has gone

she has not gone far

she may be hiding—under a mossy log
she may have run—down the serpent's hole

she may have taken flight—
but she is   always circling

she has learned who will feed her

& if this is all
you have to give

she will learn   to live
on crumbs

ii.
body: meant to bend

ode to the breaking of day

praise to you   as i begin
precious hog   generous hen

love   oh! love
yellow yolk   sizzling fat

thank you   farmer's tilling hands
tilling soil   rooting land

and equal love
for this holding mug

for clean water quenching

for zucchini's drip
—it's twining grip

the feathery carrot's fern
each spinach leaf

each red beet
resplendent   ravishing

apple strudel on the table
hot in my mouth

a bowl of oatmeal steaming
how the bowels move every morning

knowing what to keep
and what to release

determined wobble

you do not have to walk on your knees
for a hundred miles through the desert, repenting
　　　　　　　　　　　—Mary Oliver

if we could speak　　we would not
be knees　　we would be lips teeth
tongue lungs—guzzling up all the silence

we are the quiet ones
who　　from the beginning
were meant to bend

we are the begging bones
the bones of proper prayer
of vows
of skins & bruises
of ache & creak
—the genuflecting bones

if we could speak　　we would say
we are the falling bones
we would speak of how our flat faces
hit the tile　　you tumbling
—determined wobble　　learning to walk
how you tried and tried and tried again

this is not the only time
you repeated yourself
　　　in spite of pain

trying again
trying again

mostly   with men

~

if we could speak   we would speak of beauty
we would say *encore*   *encore*
to you & your ballet:
plié   pas de bourrée   grand jeté
little cat-like jumps
huge flying jumps
landing on us
bending us
to catch your fall

we remember the red-netted tutu
your brunette hair   french-twisted
—a plume   a feather there
how you loved the lipstick
you were allowed to wear
how you were always   dancing:

dancing on a stage
in a play
in the kitchen
down the hall
—performing

if we could speak   we would tell you
it wasn't all pretty   we would say

that floor
that night
the violence
you witnessed

it is over now
& you   do not
have to beg
anymore

before the dance

i gave up

dancing

(—my feet   my hips
captives of a southern

baptist slant on sin)

we didn't   dance

my date
& i

(gentle boy
        quiet boy)

he tried to understand
never said an ugly word

    ~

*what
does a young girl*

know

but   what

she is told

i was not
allowed to attend
the apartment party

where he died
falling down

stairs   he was
such a beautiful

boy:

even then
i loved a drunk

～

of the things
i've given up

nipples erect
for them:

other men
valium

the half-smile
of a slow day

i don't give a fuck

sweet   burn
blurring everything

whiskey   going

down

~

it was scotch
i had to learn

to like   but then
i liked it

way too much
& i started dancing

with everybody
with anybody

by myself
on the table

without my clothes
because the thing is:

i was flying
whirling girl

and   nobody
was going to stop

me

dancing

~

not daddy

(his   *go to hell*
religion)

not mamma

(her   *if you don't stop
i'm going to tell your daddy*)

not the preacher
—his white-hanky
spit

spraying

jesus name

over the crowd
on sunday
morning

she let herself go

This is the story of a little girl who loved to dance. She stood on her toes in the kitchen. She jumped like a cat down the hall. She marched in the den to the recording of a band playing "Seventy-six Trombones," wearing white drill-team boots and waving her baton like a twirler in the parade. She took lessons in tap and ballet. She felt beautiful and she was a lovely dancer. When she wasn't dancing, she was fidgeting. Her father would say, "Be still wiggle-worm!"

She heard her father and mother arguing all the time. Her father said her mother had done something very bad. Her mother said, "Please forgive me." Her father said, "Bitch. Whore. Fat ass." Then he hit her mother hard instead. Her mother cried until her face turned red and spit drooled out of her mouth. The little girl wet a cool cloth and washed her mother's eyes. It was the only thing she could think to do.

Every Sunday and every Wednesday they all went to the Baptist church to pray. Her mother prayed that her father wouldn't hit her anymore. She didn't know what her father prayed for, but she prayed to be a very good girl.

One day, her father said they couldn't afford dance lessons anymore. Her teacher offered to give her lessons free, but her father said no. She didn't dare cry (because very good girls don't cry). Since she was already thirteen and clearly too big to dance in the den anymore, she stopped dancing.

When she was in high school, she studied drama and made A's. It was a good substitute for dancing she thought because by now, she was growing up and trying to take her Baptist teaching that "dancing is a sin" seriously. She wanted to be a very good girl, so she went to church all the time and kept her body still and straight.

Her father said she had to be able to earn money when she was grown, so she left home to study at the university. She decided to become a teacher of drama, because her father had always said, "Mind your teachers." She thought that meant he respected them. She wanted his respect more than anything, because that would mean she was a very good girl.

Her first audition as a freshman landed her a part as a dancer in the chorus line of *Cabaret.* She was very proud. While she rehearsed the bump and grind, her body began to feel something it had never felt before. She met a boy who said he loved her. He kissed her and touched her in ways that made her want to let him kiss and touch her in places she knew were secret, places that should only be touched by her future husband. She knew from her Baptist teaching that they were guilty and had already sinned in their hearts by even wanting to be with each other in this way, so when he said, "I want to marry you," she said, "Yes," and decided to let him have her body. This is the way she became a woman.

She didn't marry that boy after all. She began to let many other boys touch her secret places. It made her feel beautiful, a little. But she was afraid all of time. She drank liquor and smoked marijuana to quiet the voice in her head that said she had done something really bad. Soon she began to accomplish things, thinking this would make her feel more like a good girl, and it did, a little.

She became one of the sexiest dancers in the *Cabaret* chorus line. She dressed herself in her new costume of lingerie, garter belt, hose, and high heels, and made her lips pout with liner and thick, red paint. The choreographer singled her out, gave her several special bit parts (even before many who called themselves dance majors). This made her feel very proud. She thought her father would be very proud too, but he must have been able to see the woman in her now, how she had been bad, because after he saw the show, the only thing he said was, "When will you change your major?"

This ruined every chance she thought she had of being a very good girl. After that, she stopped showing up for auditions. She ate all the time. Pretty soon, her breasts began to swell and her hips were full. When she went home to visit, her father said she was getting fat like her mother. She no longer felt beautiful. That's when she stopped eating altogether.

After college, she married a doctor and had a child. She thought this would always make her happy. But something in her needed more. So, she found another man who said he loved her. When he kissed her and touched her, she felt her body in ways she had never felt it before. So, she divorced her husband and married the man who made her feel. She thought this would always make her happy. But something in her needed more.

One day, she decided to audition for a musical at the community theatre. Even though she sang beautifully (the way she had sung the hymns every Sunday as a little Baptist girl), she didn't get the part. The director saw the responsible one in her and asked her to be his assistant. She was very proud. She thought this would make her husband very proud too, but her husband was furious because he wanted her at home. She decided that she could do what she wanted to do, so she did. This made her husband very angry. So, one day he said, "I don't want to live with you anymore." They separated. This made her very sad and because she no longer tried to silence the voices in her head with liquor, she was also very afraid. She was sure she had done something really bad.

Later, she came back home and begged him to forgive her because she didn't know how to support herself or how to live without him. She went to church all the time. She sang beautiful hymns in the choir. She began to teach children. She taught school, raised her children, and made a home. She was her most responsible self. She accomplished many things. She thought that being good in this way would make her happy. But something in her wanted more.

One day, she began to paint pictures and write stories because something inside of her needed to get out. Painting and writing seemed like safe, quiet activities that she could do from home where she belonged. Soon she stopped going to church. Instead, she sat on her backyard swing and listened for the voice in the trees. She could not feel her body anymore, and she never danced, and she never sang.

Soon, her feet began to ache, and she cried every day. Her stomach hurt and her body refused to receive her food.

Then one day, she read a book that said she could craft a magic box that would make her dreams come true. All she had to do was put pictures of her dreams into the box. So, she made a beautiful box and set it on her altar. She lit a candle and thought and thought, but she could not think of even one dream she wanted to come true. So, the box stayed empty. One day, she found three photographs of a beautiful dancer in arabesque, and she remembered her dream. So, she placed the photographs in the magic box and waited.

While she waited, one voice in her kept saying "Be still." She thought this was a holy voice. So, she went to sit Zen for three days. But for some reason, she could not make herself sit still. The teacher, a woman, blessed her and said, "You are good and perfect. You are more than any of this. There are many paths to holiness. Go in Peace to find the movement you really seek."

Hot tears ran down the woman's face as she received the blessing and she thought maybe the box really did have magic.

So, she went home and turned on some music. She stood on her toes in the kitchen, jumped like a cat down the hall, and moved her hips in wide open circles. Soon she began to cry. For days, she danced and cried and danced and cried. Finally, she let herself go.

While she lay on the floor sweating, her heartbeat sang in her chest. She felt the beauty of her body the way she had never felt it before, and she heard a voice saying:

You have always been a very good girl.

iii.
breath becoming

common breath

scent of cedar:

hard   red wood
resistant   to insects

brought on boats
to texas   by germans

who thought the wood
good   for building

planks   cut

for cabinets
for cabins

for chests   to protect
all things precious:

wool blanket
wedding dress

china cups
for tea
with dolls

~

this juniper   now
considered—a pest:

drinks too much
litters the landscape

blusters mustard dust in december

    ~

like you father
you and your german cut
—strong and straight

—this cedar scent:
a sign   since
    your demise
of your arriving

    ~

today   i wake
—scent of cedar   fills
the room   stinging
moist membranes

insistent
persistent

you are here

it is the day after christmas

the day after
we filled on family & food   all of us here
laughing—loud hammers cracking plastic

you were never one to join the fray

~

maybe you were crust   crisp on my tongue

maybe you were wrapping—
tossed like so many crude words

maybe you were the last carol unsung

~

what love could there be for us now
—common breath   unbroken
i do not know
yet   you are here

palpable as clay
invisible as aching

insistent
persistent

stinging

two players

in this score
we are disharmonic
—a phantom phrase

father and daughter:
violin & viola a deux

what horsehair bow
sweeps   these strings

what common breath breathes us

how many times will we sing
this dissonant refrain

when the last white line sails by

morning has dawned on these
eyes silent 18,000 times and more than
can be counted like times i've hurt someone
or times i didn't think

that many evaporated dreams have
gone like fog from a bay or
dew from morning leaves

that many dreams i've tried to
understand like love or dying
what have i learned but this:

i know nothing

nothing except the song of the frog's
throaty serenade to the night
like a mistress in black lingerie

nothing except that the cat always
gets her way   loves on her own terms
speaks her mind better than i

nothing except that time passes fast
like white lines at night on a desert highway
and no matter how i use it
there'll be none left for me
when the last line sails by
& i drift on into the dark

unfettered

nothing except that even the empire state
building and the pyramids will turn to
dust in the air like so much aged paper
you've tried to save because
it's got important headlines

nothing except that gravity and
worry wear the body down like
water carves out a canyon and that
i'm deeper now
smoother   with red-orange hues
i never thought i'd have

nothing except that long after i cannot hear
my mother's voice singing
her song will sing itself in me
on and on and on

holy water

my mother fills the vase
with water—food coloring
one drop   dropped in
red or blue   sometimes yellow

in our sparse space
grey walls   green
and gold flecked sofa
a landscape painted
by my mother's aunt
above the hi-fi

and in the dining room
there's the last supper
in ceramics: a mold
fired and painted by
my father's mother

—the two single red rose
paintings she painted
hang in the kitchen

later she will heat brown beer bottles
hang them by their necks in the kiln
until they stretch their bottoms down
and land   flat puddles of glass
on the bricks   their thin fragile stems
still stuck in the wire

and bring them to us on
sunday afternoon when she visits
and then   my father and his mother
will argue over our souls
—the southern baptist v. the church of christ

their voices rising: pitch & tone
hot like the steaming hell i imagine
we   my father   my mother & me
will surely go

my grandmother says
as though i—a child
—am not in the room

and still   my mother
sets out her vases:

holy water

molecules combined by an
unseen force & drawn from the tap
—another kind of miracle

a few thoughtful drops
common to the kitchen
used in an uncommon way
make the vases deco-art:

decanted colorist form
gracing the table
lacing the windowsill

—translucent
—stalwart
—iterations

statements of faith made

no matter how many
nights she will spend   bent over
—her sorrow spinning within her

multiples of seven

... it is better   to be whole
than to be   good ...
—John Middleton Murry

mother

will you

meet me

on the   other

side

will you

leave   your

resting head

head on over
to the pearly gates

when it is time

~

when it is time

will you

break   the veil
of understanding

like eve   (formidable
woman)   mother

lover
wife

one of us

will you meet me

   ~

will you meet me

under the tree

knowing (what

we know) and

going anyway

i hope
i never

have to see
him   again

you said
speaking of

karma

~

you left
    your body

&

me   wondering
still   whether

(or not)

love is

eternal

~

i haven't   been

good

(neither were you
    completely)

lord have mercy
christ have mercy

we tried
i am trying
still   to keep

(impossible
    commandments)

promises

to forgive

in multiples
of seven

    ~

you and your
surrender

having gone
before me

—stained
    as i am

mother

will you

meet me

on the   other

side

iv.
unbroken

shape-shifted

I Am That. I Am All. All Is Within Me.
All guides and protects me.
       —Sanskrit meaning of So Hum

crouch close

The season has shifted. A cool breeze floats through my backyard. Birds and butterflies begin their migrations through South Texas. Above me, the hawk cries, her call pierces the sky. She kettles with others—I count nine, beginning their long flight southward.

The pandemic has ended but Covid 19 still threatens, kills. Refugees flood US borders, begging for help. Politicians debate but do not resolve issues. Wildfires rage. Hurricanes make land fall. Earth quakes.

This is wilderness.

My stomach and chest ache with all these *holding vines*. I shiver with the beginnings of a mind-body breakdown. I spend large expanses of time outside, barefooted, grounding, begging earth:

oh! gentle clay
cradle & sway
these wanting bones
you are   my moor

What to do? What to do? What is one to do with all this darkness? Last night, Black Bear appeared to me in the dreamworld, a sign: go inward; be still; hibernate.

when the bear comes
carrying her dark body
& the moon has hidden behind the sky
crouch close to the fire

This is the question: how to *crouch close to the fire*. Indeed, what *is* the fire?

~

wilderness

the holding vines
grew around me
dread lock
gnarl & grip

~

this i got from the cave
where i had hidden
from the darkness

but the darkness itself
lived in that cave

~

after the misery
after the wailing

i struck a stone
& made fire

i crawled into her burning face
but she did not consume me

instead   she gave me smoke

~

soon her soot filled the cave
filled my lungs—blackening
my skin   turning to ash

my breath   becoming
the smoke and the smoking

how long i breathed this way
i do not know   my breath

my skin
my bones

became the darkness
—shapeshifted

~

my throat no longer
voiced a timid timbre

instead:

a low
guttural
rumble

now   i felt the hunger
& i began to wander

how far this wandering
would take me
or what the wandering
would give me

i did not know

~

my ears perked   attuned

i heard the pulse of earth

~

soon i tasted blood
i killed and ate
i slept and mated

but the hunger never left me

long i wandered rough terrain

desolate
desert

—dry   empty
i did not eat
i did not sleep

& the waiting
came upon me

~

after the cave and darkness
and the fire and smoke
and the wandering and the waiting

stillness
came close

~

& the stillness

fed me

~

For years, I attended worship. Sunday morning. Sunday afternoon. Sunday evening. Wednesday night prayer meetings. I memorized verses from the Bible. I was baptized, twice, and on and on I followed the rules, kneeling. I believed these teachings, their doctrines. With my entire being, I believed that following them would save me. But none of this brought me to stillness. I was lost in doing, in rule following. I had no idea how to be still.

to the thinning

There are ninety days of comings and goings, endings and beginnings for my family from August through October. In these ninety days, eighteen significant life event celebrations and anniversaries occur, among them the anniversaries of both of my parents' transitions from their fleshly bodies into their Light Bodies.

Some cultures celebrate Dia de los Muertos, Days of the Dead, on November first and second. This is a time of celebrating and honoring the ancestors. So, it seems true for many, including me, that at this time of year, the veil between the worlds thins and palpable visitations between the worlds happen.

"You must believe in life after death for this to be meaningful," you say. And I say, "I do, but not in the same way as I did when I was *Little Baptist Girl:* obedient; not the same way as I did when I was *The Recovering One:* confused; not the same way as I did when I was the *Excommunicated One:* defiant; and not the same way as I did when I was *The Reverent One:* kneeling."

Now, I believe in life after death, not because of doctrine, not because I have professed belief in one God whose sacrificial blood saves me, not because this god promises that my devotion will bring me everlasting life, not because I have followed any rules.

I believe in life after death because I have direct experiences that bring me to this *knowing:*

I sat on my bed meditating at the end of the day. I had been, for months, distraught. My granddaughter had been born during Covid and I had not been allowed to see her, an understandable and common occurrence during the pandemic. But there was more. There was an unbearable emotional distance between my daughter and me as well. In all the ways I know, I had prayed daily, sometimes hourly, I had claimed divine intervention and healing. And on this night, I had been doing just that. When I opened my eyes, I noticed a shimmering, vibrating light filling the room—not like light from a light bulb, but more like millions of particles of light, like the invisible had been made visible, like an energetic mass, not a form but a palpable, vibrating Presence. I laughed aloud, speaking to the presence, one that I assumed was the collective ancestors making their visitation. Momentarily, a tune came wafting in, one that was familiar but the title of which I could not recall. Minutes passed before the title came: "Scarlet Ribbons," a decades old song about the Holy Spirit at work to answer prayer. Again, I spoke aloud to the Presence, to them, to they—to That Into Which They Have Re-entered—to That From Which They Became incarnate as individual expressions—to That Which Exists In All Things—to That Which had somehow made Itself visible to me! Now, there came in me an unspeakable joy!

Unspeakable, effortless, spontaneous joy expressing from Within and lasting several minutes: a laughing, crying, overwhelming experience of pure joy, an experience of life after death.

~

to the fire

Today, I do not attend worship. But I do worship. I practice a multi-faith personal theology & I am making a study of silence, of stillness. Sometimes, I sit.

Sit. Breathe. Count. Chant. Breathe.
Sit. Breathe. Count. Chant. Breathe.
Give everything to the breath.
So hum. So hum. So hum.

Sometimes, I walk. Just now, the hawk calls. I run out into the sun, squinting. There! Nine hawks make their kettle, calling each other to join the ancient journey: ripples of sound, resonate, echo in this human heart and suddenly, I am shape-shifted. I am One.

As for the question of fire? For me, it is kundalini. It is ki. It is prana. It is breath. It is spirit rising within. It is here, accessible, where I am, now and where I will always be.

And I am sure that beyond appearances, there is Great Life teeming, communicating, intervening, saving, existing, being, omnipotent, omniscient, omnipresent Life Being.

to see or not to see

after A Course in Miracles

it is not my job to save the world
because the world i see is illusion

it is only my job to correct the errors
i have made   in my perception
of the world i see

what i think i see   may not be so

i set down the burden of decision

it is not my job to decide what is so
and what is not so
i have only to look   on all things
with love

that is enough

these body-eyes are not the eyes of love

but there is   one who loves
who will see
through me   for me

if i will allow it

bodies   die and decay

yet love lives

i will not look with the body's eyes
they cannot see

only love can see truly

beyond the veil of flesh and appearances
shines a light of great beauty

i will not try to hold it bound   i cannot
i can but choose   to see or not to see

the choice i make   does not dim the light at all
because in truth i am the light   and not the darkness i have seen
this light is all that i am in truth

let the moment come

when all that i am is
all that i see

say this

i am of an age   that if i died today
you might say   *she died too young*
when   in a decade you might say
she lived a good   long life

i say   *why say anything at all*
about how i've lived beyond this
—patch of wildflowers

today:
verbena bloom
sudden rise of wild petunia
redbud   better now
since i pruned away
what winter wasted

she is a summer lover   like me
& tho her magenta show each spring
begins unwinding winter's dark core
& from my window as i watch her bloom
    i am warmed

i do not shed my wool and down
until the summer rains have come
and toads begin to sing

when the redbud dips and bows
her magenta head in the cumulous breeze
& white clouds are climbing vines in a cerulean sky

i am a barefoot child—adoring life

everyday miracles:

two thousand seeds in each sunflower's face
neon yellow aphids on the milkweed stem
the beat of hummingbird wings
—seventy beats each second

how she carries dandelion down
in her beak to her nest
how the brown squirrel hangs upside down

how he and three others frolic & romp
lounge about without a care

how i am smiling now

remember this

say   this

supreme being

we are the state of complete expansion
all possibility existing
pure consciousness

—pulse of existence

we are the undoing & the undone
at rest   not void
pure potentiality

here we are one unified mass
undivided
pervasive

all light within us

unbroken
unspoken
boundless
desireless
nameless

neither object nor thought

intelligence teeming
    a hover
    a hum

all sound   unsounding
resounding
resounding

love

breath of the cosmos

now is now is now again
now is now until the end
and there is no end
and there is no end

here is here and here again
here is here until the end
and there is no end
and there is no end

light slips in for a moment or two
light slips into me   to you
light slips out   back into light
light becomes light becomes light becomes light

breath of the body—common breath
breath of the cosmos back to breath
what has become remains it still
still as it is and always will

be what it is   it is   it is
nothing goes   nothing stays
formless formless formless form
is here is here is here is now

light and breath and body bow

and there is no end
and there is no end

blessing

for my children

may love beyond measure fill your heart
may it open wide with thanksgiving
let there be ease and understanding

may the waters of your being rise within you
seeping the energy of your soul's purpose out
through your pores until you overflow
with joy and gratitude for all that is given

may you know the goodness of your own heart
and every beautiful thing that you are
yet   let the thorny rose bloom around you
scenting your every desire   and warning
warning anyone who would harm you

may you know your own power at its source

let your busy hands rest from their doing
let delight occupy your mind
let your soul sing free from worry and striving
let your eyes open to your own preciousness
and the preciousness of time
may you know that it is now
and now   and now again
without end

may the flesh you inhabit serve you well
breathing and moving with great ease and strength

may you know peace
may you teach peace
may you love in peace

may all that you are and all that you will become
be as it should be:

perfect
whole
complete

About the Author

d. ellis phelps' poems, essays, and visual art have appeared widely online and in print. As an educator, she has taught fine arts in various venues with students of all ages for decades.

She is the author of four poetry collections: *of failure & faith* and *words gone wild* (Kelsay Books, 2023 and 2021), *what she holds* (Moon Shadow Sanctuary Press, 2020), *what holds her* (Main Street Rag, 2019), and of the novel *Making Room for George* (Moon Shadow Sanctuary Press, 2016). She is the prize-winning editor of more than a dozen anthologies and the founding editor of *formidable Woman sanctuary* and of *fws: international journal of literature & art,* both digital publications.

Find more about her here:
www.dellisphelps.com

About the Cover Artist

Esther van Overbeek is a Dutch self-taught photographer who once started with macro photography. She is now award-winning and an expert in the field of multiple exposures, inspired by Monet and Van Gogh.

Find more on her website:
www.esthersfotografie.nl

www.ingramcontent.com/pod-product-compliance
Lightning Source LLC
Chambersburg PA
CBHW071226160426
43196CB00012B/2428